D0930245

DATE DUE

96238

MONSTER WHEELS

Bill Holder & Harry Dunn

 Sterling Publishing Co., Inc. New York

This book is dedicated to the drivers and crewmen of the nation's big trucks. The authors thank them for their help in the preparation of this book.

Library of Congress Cataloging-in-Publication Data

Holder, William G., 1937–
  Monster wheels.

  Summary: A look, in text and illustrations, a variety
of monster trucks doing tricks and stunts.
  1. Monster trucks—Juvenile literature. [1. Monster
trucks. 2. Trucks] I. Dunn, Harry. II. Title.
TL230.15.H65 1990   629.224   89-26170

  ISBN 0-8069-5844-8 paper

1   3   5   7   9   10   8   6   4   2

Published in 1990 by Sterling Publishing Company, Inc.
387 Park Avenue South, New York, N.Y. 10016
First published in paperback by Willowisp Press, Inc., Ohio
© 1987 Willowisp Press, Inc.
Distributed in Canada by Sterling Publishing
% Canadian Manda Group, P.O. Box 920, Station U
Toronto, Ontario, Canada M8Z 5P9
Distributed in Great Britain and Europe by Cassell PLC
Artillery House, Artillery Row, London SW1P 1RT, England
Distributed in Australia by Capricorn Ltd.
P.O. Box 665, Lane Cove, NSW 2066
Manufactured in the United States of America
All rights reserved

Table of Contents

Imagine yourself behind the wheel of one of the world's most powerful trucks! You are so high off the ground that you feel as if you are 14 feet tall. Four huge tires carry the truck's monster body. The power of the engine surges beneath your hands. The noise almost shatters your ears as the truck moves ahead. With the truck's incredible power, you could crush anything in sight!

You've just entered BIG-WHEEL TRUCK COUNTRY!

Big-wheel trucks are thrilling to see! Their stunning paint jobs and shiny chrome attract everyone's attention. People from all over come to see these trucks do their incredible stunts!

The very first monster machine was BIGFOOT®. Bob Chandler owns a four-wheel drive shop and he built BIGFOOT® so that he could drive off-road over any kind of obstacle. Bob crushed some cars with his truck one day just for fun and the idea caught on. Today, these monster mashers are everywhere, and they can do just about anything!

Bob liked his first BIGFOOT® truck so much that he built several more. There are now several different BIGFOOT® trucks out there performing and there are sure to be more in the future.

Tall trucks come in just about every shape and size. Some of these crazy trucks aren't trucks at all. They are really car bodies mounted on big wheels.

The VIRGINIA BEACH BEAST® is a really strange-looking truck. It uses tracks instead of big tires. It moves along like an army tank.

8

These trucks not only look weird, they have strange names. Some of the strange names are THUMPER, KING KRUNCH, AWESOME KONG, and ICE MONSTER. With names like these, you can be sure to expect a thrilling show!

The truck monsters perform all kinds of death-defying tricks. But almost everyone likes car crushing the best. Fans love to hear the sound of crushing metal and cracking glass as these huge trucks smash cars as flat as pancakes.

Most of the trucks stop once they are on top of the cars. The drivers then usually open the doors of their trucks, stand up, and wave to the crowd.

Watching the monster trucks get on top of the cars to crush them is almost as exciting as the crushing itself. Some trucks simply move up and crawl over the cars. Other trucks back up over the cars. Still other trucks start from a short distance away and gather power as they come near the cars. Then they attack the cars with a mighty crush!

CAR CRUSHING IS A DANGEROUS BUSINESS!

Car crushing may look easy to the fans, but it is very dangerous for the drivers. The drivers have to be very careful when they are crushing cars so that their trucks don't tip over.

The cars that the drivers crush need to be the same size and style so that they will all collapse evenly. Most of the drivers either chock or puncture the car tires so that the cars will not move when the big truck rolls over them.

Some of these truck monsters have even crushed school buses! This trick is very dangerous. Only a few tall trucks have been able to do it. It is a long fall to the ground if the truck should fall off the edge of the buses.

A wheelie, also called a wheelstand, is an incredible sight! The giant truck pulls its front wheels up into the air as it is moving. Some of the truck monsters have even done wheelstanding with their back wheels instead of their front ones up in the air!

But doing these high-rise stunts is very dangerous. The trucks can turn over backward if the driver is not careful. The heavy roll cages built around the truck cabs protect the drivers if the truck should roll. Many drivers also wear protective helmets and carry fire extinguishers.

These daredevil truck monsters also race through giant mud pits. This sport is called mud bogging. The giant wheels help the trucks get through the gooey mush. Afterward, the mud covers nearly every part of the vehicle. Can you imagine how many hours it takes to get these trucks looking clean and proud again?

The fans of these giant trucks are always looking for chilling new tricks. The daring drivers will do just about anything—the more dangerous the better! Each one of them wants to be the first one to try a new trick.

Some drivers hook their trucks up to weights and pull them. These weights weigh many tons and it takes all the power these trucks have to pull them. Sometimes the trucks buck like wild horses because of the weights.

Other drivers even take their trucks through water. The trucks float like corks because of their huge tires. But water trips are not as easy as they look. The famous BEARFOOT® truck made a water trip with eight tires on its body. But another truck turned completely over. Only the tops of its tires showed when the truck went under water.

Another thrill for fans is watching these trucks climb hills. One truck, the ICE MONSTER JR., even climbs a hill made of ice!

Obstacle course races give the trucks and drivers the chance to try all their tricks. The course has several different jobs for the trucks to do. Sometimes the monster trucks have to pull a weight, do some tight turning, run through the mud, or go up and down hills. The trucks move at a thrilling pace from one obstacle to another. The first one to complete all of the obstacles is the winner!

23

The trucks need all the power they can get to do their incredible stunts. Most of these trucks use powerful eight-cylinder car engines to turn their four giant tires. These engines are the biggest car motors that have ever been built!

Some motors use superchargers to force more air into the motors and make them more powerful. Some of the tall trucks even use two engines to create more power. And one of the huge trucks even uses an old aircraft engine for power!

What makes these trucks really different is their big tires. These amazing tires help the trucks do their daredevil stunts—from crushing cars to standing high in the air.

Most of the trucks use tires that are five and one-half feet high. That's just a little shorter than most grown-ups! One of the famous BIGFOOT® trucks even has tires that are ten feet high. Sometimes, this truck uses eight giant tires at once.

You might think that there is a lot of air in these big tires. But the giant tires carry only about six to eight pounds of air. A car tire carries about 30 pounds. Monster truck tires are big and heavy and weigh hundreds of pounds.

Heavy springs help the trucks to sit up high. To keep the trucks from bouncing, many of the trucks use twenty or more shock absorbers!

96238

ILLINOIS PRAIRIE DISTRICT LIBRARY

It's not easy to move the giant trucks to different parts of the country for the shows that they perform. Many of the trucks are too tall and too wide to be driven on the street. The tires of these trucks are stored on trailers and the trucks are carried sitting on small tires. The trucks look really strange without their big tires.

Some fans like these trucks so much that they wear T-shirts or hats with their favorite trucks on them! At a truck event, you can take home all kinds of souvenirs! And you can take with you the memories of the thrilling world of these incredible trucks.

GLOSSARY

Car Crushing—A big-wheel truck trick in which the trucks drive up on top of a number of cars and flatten them. This was the first trick that big wheel trucks performed.

Mud Bogging—Driving a big-wheel truck through a pit where the mud might be as deep as four feet.

Obstacle Course—A race where the big-wheel trucks perform several different tasks.

Roll Cage—Special steel bars in the cab of a big-wheel truck that protect the driver if the truck should overturn.

Wheelies—A trick in which truck monsters pull their front or back two wheels off the ground as they are moving. Also called wheelstanding.

Index